Suicide. An unholy exit from the roller coaster we call life. A global claimant of around 2,000 souls per day. In a world rampant with stressors, pressures, and seemingly endless trials, it can be a challenge to find a silver lining among what feels like chaos.

I've had trials and caved into various temptations, and throughout my struggles, have been able to experience God's still and soft truths in action. *A true game changer.*

I hope you're along for this ride with me, as I take you through some of the lowest points in my life, and the way God broke through the tragic state of my mind and surroundings and reminded me of the tools that everyone needs in order to *live abundantly*. I'm not talking about money or property. I'm talking about the abundant life that Jesus came to give us all: Freedom. Salvation. *Joy.*

Let's talk about two of the main ways Satan employs his demons into our space (*if we let him*) to steal our joy and challenge our freedom: **Idols and Lies**. In the following chapters, you'll get a glimpse at how these dark elements can be used to bring about depression and steer minds towards making rash, unreasonable decisions—and ultimately for some, ideate over suicide.

Although it was a whirlwind experience to endure the trials I am about to share with you, I praise God for the perfect opportunity to minister to His people. It is my hope that you or a loved one will be able to glean wisdom by the hearing of my own trials, and perhaps together, you and I can...

KILL
SUICIDE
IN 3 CHAPTERS

THE CURE FOR DEPRESSION & ANXIETY

CHAPTER ONE
THE IDOLS

IDOLATRY.

Whether we see it or not, our world is wrought with it. Sure, folks aren't peddling golden calves and Asherah poles anymore, but that doesn't mean the enemy didn't find a new trick to pull on our generation...

Picture this, the model of a perfect family. Husband with his wife, kids, and a beautiful home, somewhere on a secluded patch of land to call their own. It's what I desired in my heart of hearts, more than anything in the world, for a long, long time. Or how about the dream spouse? You had every detail hand-picked already in your mind. Meanwhile your friends are all getting married and magically winding up with their custom-dreamt fairy tale prince/princess charmings. But you somehow, got stuck with...*whoever this is*. Been there, done that too.

The point I'm making is, idolatry can stem from anywhere, and is Satan's prime mental disease he uses to inflict mankind:

"Mortify therefore your members which are upon the earth; fornication, uncleanness, inordinate affection, evil concupiscence, and covetousness, which is idolatry:" Colossians 3:5 KJV

These idols, when served by our hearts, require constant attention and sacrifice on our part to maintain:

Idol of Sexual Pleasure? ... *Waste time and money, "swiping right" on dating apps, whilst hitting the club every weekend.*

Idol of Money? ... *Withhold your tithes while taking every job known to man.*

One would soon find it's a lot more work to keep these pleasure-inducing idols happy, than to simply have none to begin with.

"Their sorrows shall be multiplied that hasten after another god: Their drink offerings of blood will I not offer, Nor take up their names into my lips."
Psalm 16:4 KJV

The agenda of an idol is always the same: To claim us, while simultaneously convincing us that we claim them. But enough beating around hypotheticals, let's talk testimony; for out of the innumerable idols I've created in my life, none were as gripping as the one I fashioned out of a woman, with whom I was *madly in love with...*

———————

It's somewhere in the year of 2013. I'm roughing it by myself in Los Angeles, three-thousand miles from home… *but not to me.* You see in my mind, I *was* home. As at home as home could ever be and more. Because *she* was out here too. *She* happened to be my best friend. At one point we were each others' closest friends, and that built a camaraderie that would inspire me to make the move out west, tailing right behind her.

We'd go to movies, heckle our peers, but most of all...create stories. We were both writers, you see, *"taking Hollywood by storm"*. There came a time when my affections

would rise again *(yes, again)* towards her, and I couldn't
shake the suspicion that she had some hidden feelings for
me as well.

...Either way, I was determined to get them out.

———————

It was Valentine's Day. A spontaneous delivery of
"Friendship Flowers" had worked pretty well in the past,
but I didn't want to come on too strong. It was after all,
Valentine's Day. I had already burned a bridge with her
once, and so was determined to maintain our friendship
this time.

…So, I shot her a text. Something encouraging, or sweet. I
can't remember.

No response…

Hours went by. I panicked, thinking, *"Great going, Daniel.
You came on too strong, and now she's ignoring you."*
I texted her again, hoping to clear the air. To which I was
just ignored, yet again.
In truth, I had no idea if I was being ignored or if she just
hadn't seen the text yet, but by then, the paranoia had
already settled in.

...I think I might've even texted her *again.*

The entirety of Valentine's Day went by. The damage was
done. The texts were definitely seen *(who goes a day without
checking their phone)*, and I was indeed, ignored. Only now,

thanks to the series of repeatedly unanswered messages, I looked like a psychopath.

I didn't get it. Well, I did, but I also...*didn't.* There was so much that didn't add up. That kiss on the cheek she gave me before she moved away, the time she invited me to share a hotel room *(I don't recommend that)* over a random vacation...the fact that I at one point was one of her closest friends.

...Why didn't she *want me?*

I reasoned in my mind, after a constant grapple between the real and the insane, that she must have been afraid to lose me in the same way she had lost so many of her previous romantic partners...maybe she loved me *that much.* It was a dangerous thought. A wild assumption. A good one to me at the time, but still a wild card to toss out there.

...I ran with it.

And so alone, scared, and 3,000 miles from home, I did what *anyone* tormented by a non-responsive idol would do: *...I bought an engagement ring.*

By now, suicidal ideation had become an all too familiar stream of thought. I must've been hitting a low point every single day. I struggled with pornography, using it as a drug-hit to float my emotions, and as soon as life would get tough, or work would take its toll, I had no foundation to uphold my spirits. I stood on nothing, because the one thing I was pursuing, was rejecting me. It's after all what idols do after a while...but I didn't know this yet. I didn't know how *she* was being used in my mind, as Satan's plot to *kill me.*

The ring was in hand. My nerves wouldn't allow me to pop the question in person, so in typical 22-year-old fashion, I shot her another text, with a picture of the ring, hoping that by the slimmest of all chances, I had pegged her correctly. In my mind, this was my last hope at any chance of joy.

...She called my family.

It's midnight in the middle of the vast, strange, and wild west. There I was, alone in my rented cubicle, on the 31st floor of one of the tallest skyscrapers in Downtown Los Angeles. I had already scouted the lookout deck a few floors down, just to see if a fall from that height would indeed *get the job done...*

If not for the immediate response of my mother, hopping on the soonest flight out to California, I might've actually taken my life. I was in a spiral that had taken me so far down, I mistook even darkness for the light.

My mother stuck with me for days, which turned into weeks. By the arduous passage of time, the dust had finally settled. It was then that *mental illness* would become an all too familiar topic around the house. I was even taken to see a counselor...but there was something I suspected, even back then. I could easily recall a time when I wasn't plagued by the painful *need* for my idols, driving me to the point of suicidal ideation. I had a lot of passions and interests...things I was good at. Things that brought me joy, especially when devoted to the Lord. Although I didn't know it yet, the rising chatter of mental illness among my loved ones would soon take me down an even *darker* dive...

CHAPTER TWO

THE LIES

THE SERPENT was more subtil than

any beast of the field which the LORD God had made. And he said unto the woman, Yea, hath God said, Ye shall not eat of every tree of the garden? And the woman said unto the serpent, We may eat of the fruit of the trees of the garden: but of the fruit of the tree which is in the midst of the garden, God hath said, Ye shall not eat of it, neither shall ye touch it, lest ye die. And the serpent said unto the woman, Ye shall not surely die: for God doth know that in the day ye eat thereof, then your eyes shall be opened, and ye shall be as gods, knowing good and evil. And when the woman saw that the tree was good for food, and that it was pleasant to the eyes, and a tree to be desired to make one wise, she took of the fruit thereof, and did eat, and gave also unto her husband with her; and he did eat. And the eyes of them both were opened, and they knew that they were naked; and they sewed fig leaves together, and made themselves aprons. And they heard the voice of the LORD God walking in the garden in the cool of the day: and Adam and his wife hid themselves from the presence of the LORD God amongst the trees of the garden."
Genesis 3:1-8 KJV

Satan is the Father of All Lies (John 8:44) and uses lies as his primary weapon against humanity. In the example earlier, we witness Satan's cunning strategy to trick us into accepting false claims: **cover lies in truth.** This is diabolically effective. Satan specifically followed up his lie, stating *"Ye shall not surely die"*, with something that was in fact true: *"your eyes shall be opened, ... knowing good and evil"*.

In the same way, Satan sought to plant a lie amid my loved ones, my family, and even me. His objective, a secret, though more insidious than any of us could've ever imagined. I had made some rash decisions in Los Angeles. I'm sure I worried a lot of people—while building a lifestyle fueled by sexual immorality...all of that was true.

...But I wasn't crazy.

It was about 1 o'clock. Seven years had passed since my little Californian misadventure. I was married to my high school sweetheart, had four kids, and a schedule stacked sky-high. I knew I needed to get a good amount of writing done, so I planned to seclude myself in peace and quiet for the rest of the day. What could possibly go wrong?

Boom. Just like that, my 10-month-old screams like bloody murder. She was placed on the floor. Heaven forbid, anyone, place her on the floor. My wife scrambles to finish the dishes with her newly released pair of arms as our sons watch their little sister fall out in the middle of the kitchen.

I quicken my pace over, picking her up. I give her the classic "Ah, ah, ah", but the little girl's not having it. We go out the garage door for some outside time. It calms her down for a second...but only a second—
"WAAAHH!!!", she pleads.

I close the door, hoping not to alarm the neighborhood, and like any decent brick-head, take this as an opportunity to lay down a good ole' father-daughter authority session.

After a few minutes of getting about as far as anyone would with a 10-month-old baby, my wife walks into the garage. And now, I'm in trouble. I was immediately tense. I felt disrespected, even. And so we argue, with the screaming baby in hand. Until my mother walks in, asking me to please just *"let it go"*.

It should've been the end of it. I could've taken that as a cue to complete my writing at the public library...unfortunately, *I did not*.

Now, since Los Angeles, a lot about me had changed. I quit my job, moved back east, and even reconnected with my old church. It was a full one-eighty—I was a new man. A new man, however, that still struggled with pornography...

Amid handing my daughter off to whoever would take her, I proceeded to enact what many in the house had come to know as my trademark *"outbursts"*. These were not pretty. I went to thrashing, banging, and kicking stuff in the garage while screaming my points at the peak volume of what was humanly possible. I even kicked so hard, I chipped off a piece of flesh from my shin *(which took over a month to heal)*. I screamed in my mother's and my wife's faces—as was my custom to treat opponents at times like this, whilst losing all control of projectile spit flying from my teeth.

It was...*demonic.*

But to understand this moment, we need to rewind a couple of days...

——————

It's Tuesday afternoon of that exact same week. I'm sitting in my car. Just had a huge job change, so I'm feeling the stress and trying to kill some time by getting back to some writing that I had put down about a month ago… But I just can't bring myself to write. I can't get my mind off of work...off of money. And I begin to feel, more or less, miserable.

Now, I've long confessed my failures to pornography to my wife, and have been blessed to have a partner that will encourage me to do better, with every mishap...*but that didn't stop me.*

I pulled out my phone and *went in on* some watered-down, non-committal, in-and-out, soft-core porn. And immediately as I *finished*, I felt an invisible "wind" (*this is hard to explain*), like an evil force, rushing into my forehead. This was a very familiar feeling. Happens every time. It wasn't like a headache, though it felt as if something pure evil had just entered my body, through a hole in my forehead, right between my eyes. Like the mall just opened its doors on Black Friday, and a mob of people just rushed in. I felt like the mall that had just opened its doors.

...To demons.

And apparently, as many of them as could legally enter my body, by way of my freshly committed sin.

"For we wrestle not against flesh and blood, but against principalities, against powers, against the rulers of the darkness of this world, against spiritual wickedness in high places."
Ephesians 6:12 KJV

Sin opens the door to demonic forces, in your house, in your life, and even in your body. What would happen in the days that followed this sin are the effects of the demonic influence in my life:

Extreme guilt.
Impatience.
Isolation.
Stubbornness.

...And finally, *rage.*

It was a demon hiding in plain sight, only manifesting when it would appear like a regular emotional reaction. I was blinded to all of this for years, going along with our contemporary stream of thought, thinking it was simply a need for my surroundings to change. My family began to chatter once again about mental illness, petitioning me to see another counselor. I laid low, trying to earn their good graces back, but it was no use. We were all fed up. This cycle of outbursts had a distressing recurrence that was impossible to deny, like clockwork. I had already been arrested once and was sent to state-mandated anger management. There was almost nothing left to do but get diagnosed, so I could be put on medication.

...I told you it would get dark.

A morning or two later, I sat up in the room my wife and I shared with our kids, repenting aloud for my sins to the lust of the flesh—as a revelation simultaneously dawned upon me. The pattern of my outbursts matched the exact pattern of my failures to pornography: Once every month.

———————

Mental illness, I'd love to break it to you, is a demonic construct. There is no such thing. It is a veil to hide demonic activity, so that it may continue its work in the shadows. What sense does it make for an *illness* to exist, that inhibits the moral ability of some but not others?

"for all have sinned and fall short of the glory of God, being justified freely by His grace through the redemption that is in Christ Jesus,"
Romans 3:23-24 NKJV

Sin...is the true illness. And we *all* need a cure. The *only* cure is the Blood of Jesus Christ.

You may have heard about Genetic Mental Disorders, like schizophrenia or bipolar, lying dormant until adulthood in the children of parents who also suffered from the same thing. But I'm here to tell you (*if you can accept it*) that the entire idea of there being a "gene" motivating these issues is simply man's attempt to naturally explain the supernatural. Genetic Mental Disorders are a veil...*a lie*, concocted by the enemy to conceal his ***hollow attempts*** to bring down family trees with the exact same tricks that worked on one's ancestors. Demons, moving on from father or mother—to son or daughter. Making the stronghold of mental illness a pre-meditated demonic attack in the spiritual dimension, utilizing lies, idols, or *both*.

 If this information is making you upset...*you're on the right track*, because Satan's primary advantage is gained through deception...*and he lied to us all*. It's enough to make anyone mad.

If the enemy can get us to swallow his lies, he can continue his work in the background, undetected. What's worse, we won't even be awakened to the sins that may have invited his demons in the first place *(as was the case in my addiction to pornography)*. But what's *even* worse, Satan will have a new edge of attack, emboldened by the unfortunately negative stigma, surrounding mental illness: inadequacy...disability...*illness*. As a survivor of the onslaught of negative messaging once one is labeled as "mentally ill", I can tell you that one of the most significant contributors to my thoughts of committing suicide were the deceptive feelings of invalidity made bold by loved ones, counselors, and even family members who are more convinced of the secular clinical view, rather than exposing what is really a demonic attack; a demonic attack...*that can be fought back*.

"For God hath not given us the spirit of fear; but of power, and of love, and of a **sound mind**."
2 Timothy 1:7 KJV

I can't even count the number of times those horrible lies of illness and invalidity, spoken right to my heart, used to drive my mind to suicidal ideation.

So, when these lies are swarming all around and you can't break free; when there seems as if there's none you can turn to, confide in, or even sit down with to escape the inescapable and sometimes manic torrent of degrading thoughts...what do you do? ... Where do you go?

CHAPTER THREE
THE SOLUTION

IT'S LATE SPRING,

sometime within the mid-morning. My world was swirling around me. Right was left, up was down. I was disillusioned and losing my very faith in God. Who knows the origin of the voice I just heard in prayer...whether it was God, the Devil, or just plain old *me*, I know I didn't like what it said. I needed clarity. I needed peace.

Although I didn't know it yet, I was clutching a huge idol, hugging it close to my chest. I had carried this little golden trinket around for years, as it silently guided almost every decision I ever made.

...Fear.

The depression had long set in. I wanted to look at porn. Suicidal thoughts were abound. Desperate, and as a last-ditch effort to maintain my righteousness and my sanity, I flicked on a playlist of worship music—

…The atmosphere immediately shifted.

Raging emotions began to settle, tempering under a new dialogue. Like a leaf-bearing dove, the soft acoustic intro of *The Heart of Worship* filled my ears...

I began to sing...then I stood. Before I knew it, I was swaying back and forth, lifting my arms to Heaven, as the weightiest depression I'd had in a while evaporated like snow in the spring.

It was *miraculous.*

"O come, let us sing unto the LORD: Let us make a joyful noise to the rock of our salvation. Let us come before his presence with thanksgiving, And make a joyful noise unto him with psalms. For the LORD is a great God, And a great King above all gods. In his hand are the deep places of the earth: The strength of the hills is his also. The sea is his, and he made it: And his hands formed the dry land. O come, let us worship and bow down: Let us kneel before the LORD our maker."
Psalm 95:1-6 KJV

And that's when I realized it...*worship*. Worship is the key. Worship tempers our hearts, not only to accept the fact that the rigors of our lives all nestle within the capable hands of an almighty God, but also to pass the Lord our worries like a sacrifice upon an altar. A lump enlarged inside of my throat as my eyes began to water, and all of time for a moment, ceased to exist. It was climactic, it was cathartic, it was dare I say...*euphoric*. I wept, there alone in my parents' attic, loud and unrelenting, as my head bent to the floor, tears streaming from my face, as I realized...I had made fear, my god. No more. As the next song rang out, I sang those perfectly timed lyrics, making them my solemn declaration that I'd no longer be a slave to fear. For I, was a child of God.

As my heart went from the depths of depression and suicidal ideation, to filling to overflowing with a deep-set and long-lasting joy in a matter of 20 minutes, it dawned upon me, that I would never be forgetting this moment; this scene of me worshipping the Lord all by myself in my parents' attic. It was then that a burden engrained itself within my heart, to share with all what I had learned.

———————

I'd love to give you a 5-step guide at this point. Shucks, I'd even take 3-steps. But the truth is, there is only <u>one way</u> to truly *kill* suicide. And it's easier than expensive therapy sessions, and more effective than what you'll find at your local pharmacy. It's worship. **True worship will pierce the enemy's lies, and help you slay even the tallest of idols.** I recommend finding a quiet place alone, where you won't be tempted to worry about what others are thinking. God will do an emergency surgery on your heart if you let Him, while lifting a hundred pounds from your shoulders.

———————

Of course, as time draws on, the Devil may get crafty, *as he did with me.* Devising lies, and tugging at idols, to the point where the heart may feel unwilling to submit to a worship session. At times like this, I would suggest that:

> **A:** If it is an **<u>idol</u>** you're struggling with, pour through scripture to remind yourself of where God's rightful place ought to be in our hearts:

"Therefore I say to you, do not worry about your life, what you will eat or what you will drink; nor about your body, what you will put on. Is not life more than food and the body more than clothing? Look at the birds of the air, for they neither sow nor reap nor gather into barns; yet your heavenly Father feeds them. Are you not of more value

than they? Which of you by worrying can add one cubit to his stature? "So why do you worry about clothing? Consider the lilies of the field, how they grow: they neither toil nor spin; and yet I say to you that even Solomon in all his glory was not arrayed like one of these. Now if God so clothes the grass of the field, which today is, and tomorrow is thrown into the oven, will He not much more clothe you, O you of little faith? "Therefore do not worry, saying, 'What shall we eat?' or 'What shall we drink?' or 'What shall we wear?' For after all these things the Gentiles seek. For your heavenly Father knows that you need all these things. But seek first the kingdom of God and His righteousness, and all these things shall be added to you. Therefore do not worry about tomorrow, for tomorrow will worry about its own things. Sufficient for the day is its own trouble."
Matthew 6:25-34 NKJV

"And every one that hath forsaken houses, or brethren, or sisters, or father, or mother, or wife, or children, or lands, for my name's sake, shall receive an hundredfold, and shall inherit everlasting life."
Matthew 19:29 KJV

"And he was withdrawn from them about a stone's cast, and kneeled down, and prayed, saying, Father, if thou be willing, remove this cup from me: nevertheless not my will, but thine, be done."
Luke 22:41-42 KJV

Or:

B: If it is a <u>lie</u> (*or a message that steals your peace*) that plagues you, test it by God's word; *giving it no space in your mind until it passes this test.* Here are 3 scriptures that can shut down the numerous lies of the enemy:

"For God sent not his Son into the world to condemn the world; but that the world through him might be saved."
John 3:17 KJV

"For God is not the author of confusion, but of peace, as in all churches of the saints."
1 Corinthians 14:33 KJV

"For God hath not given us the spirit of fear; but of power, and of love, and of a **sound mind**."
2 Timothy 1:7 KJV

After you've done that, don't be afraid to rock-out, all alone with the Lord God Almighty. He loves to hear our praise and inhabits the praises of his people (Psalm 22:3). What better company to keep when you're feeling down, than the sovereign Creator of the Universe, who loves us more than we can understand?

I suggest beginning _each day_ with a prayer/worship session of whatever length you desire.

If you have a friend that has struggled with suicidal thoughts, first pray for them. Command aloud that by the power of the Blood of Jesus all demons must retreat into the outer darkness. Then, please, hand them this book. If this testimony has made a difference for you today, then praise God, you can be confident it will make a difference for them.

Anything is a step to more victories.

———————

If you or a loved one has struggled with demonic oppression, possession, addiction, or dependency of any kind, *please* read **Quit Porn in 3 Chapters** for a full account detailing the <u>removal</u> of a powerful evil spirit, and the sinful habits that brought it along in the first place.

MUSIC RESOURCES
SONGS FOR WORSHIP & PRAYER

If you're looking for material to start building a worship album, look no further. Below are songs from my personal playlist. These songs have paced some of the most authentic solo prayer and worship sessions I've ever had.

(Of course, I'll also acknowledge the numerous styles of worship music out there, and that we all may have our own unique expression of praise.)

The Heart of Worship, Live - *Passion, Matt Redman*

Spirit of the Living God - *Vertical Worship*

No Longer Slaves (Spontaneous) - *Bethel Music*

So Will I (100 Billion X), Live - *Hillsong Worship*

Bigger Than I thought - *Sean Curran*

All Praise, Live - *Sean Curran*

Awesome God, Live - *Hillsong UNITED*

10,000 Reasons (Bless the Lord) - *Matt Redman*

Oceans (Where Feet may Fail) - *Hillsong UNITED*

Oceans (Where Feet May Fail) - *Rend Collective*

How He Loves, Live - *Passion, Crowder*

Here I Am to Worship - *The Worship Initiative, Shane & Shane*

True North - *Rend Collective*

How He Loves Us - *The Worship Initiative, Shane & Shane*

Graves Into Gardens (Live) - *Elevation Worship, Brandon Lake*

Better is One Day - *The Worship Initiative, Shane & Shane*

Blessed Be Your Name - *The Worship Initiative, Shane & Shane*

The Holy Spirit has often whispered solutions to the most puzzling dilemmas and exposed my most hidden weaknesses during worship sessions. Don't be afraid to *flick it on* at a moment's notice.